CW00434852

The Pursuit of Success

Your Grades Don't Define You

Chantel Brooks

Copyright © 2023 by Chantel Brooks

All rights reserved.

No part of this publication may be produced, distributed, or transmitted in any form or by any means, including photocopying, recording, or other electronic or mechanical methods, without the prior written permission of the publisher, except in the case of brief quotations embodied in critical reviews and certain other non-commercial uses permitted by copyright law.

For permission requests reach out to:

www.thepursuitofsuccess.co.uk

Permissions Coordinator at the email address below:

sales@thepursuitofsuccess.co.uk

Life and Success Media Ltd

e-mail: info@abookinsideyou.com

www.abookinsideyou.com

ISBN Number: 978-1-399961-61-5

I dedicate this book to an amazing friend and mentor who has literally been with me throughout my journey of becoming a teacher and beyond. She has been a mentor, advisor, supporter and has helped to open some doors for me throughout. She has been an inspiration to me and a rock. She has seen me through good and bad times in my career and has still supported me to this day, Val Taylor, I salute you and thank you.

Foreword

"Words are the halfway house to lost things"
(Sigmund Freud)

I have known Chantel for many years. My first encounter was when she was my student on a top-up degree so it's a particular pleasure to be invited to prepare this 'appetiser' for her work. I was struck from our first meeting by her determination and it was not just a determination to be personally successful, but rather, it was a determination to make a difference, to have an impact, to make things better. As the Ballad Singer in Bertolt Brecht's play *The Causacian Chalk Circle* exclaims, "Terrible is the temptation to do good"! My subsequent dealings with Chantel have always been encounters with her various projects and all directed towards making things better for others and particularly those disadvantaged or struggling. This is a real theme.

This book is devoted to gathering together some of that energy and experience in order that even more people might benefit from her presence, personality and determination. When I'm asked, as a writer, by those who wish to publish their work for advice, I always remind these prospective writers that they're asking the wrong question. You do not become a writer by being published; you become a writer by writing, by having the courage to 'show' your feelings, thoughts and opinions. This is a fact, but for those of us who do publish, the context is made easier by all of those people who want to write but don't. And the most common reason for would-be writers not writing (like not doing anything) is that feeling we might not be good enough, talented enough, clever enough. And the most damaging thing this imposter culture does is that it stops us trying and this is what Chantel's story counteracts. As the poet T S Eliot wisely said, "For us there is only the trying. The rest is not our business".

Chantel has had her share of knockbacks, frustrations and disappointments as we all have, but it doesn't stop her trying and going again. In a world obsessed with superficial achievements as opposed to those harder, deeper values like integrity, commitment and learning, it is refreshing to return to an account education as centrally engaged with individuals. Biesta surely had it right when he described education as "the situation or process which provides opportunity for individuals to come into presence, that is, to show who they are and where they stand."

This is what Chantel's story really tells us, that we have to own our own education as we need to own our own lives and that we always have choices and we need to learn to make them. And that means we need support and certainly a better education system than we have, but it also means we need one another and need to share our experiences and need to value our stories. This is what Chantel has done on our behalf as an example not only of perseverance against the odds but also of the value of finding our voices. As Domanique, one of this year's Foundation students wrote in her journal: "We are all given a voice to speak and I feel we should use it".

Chantel never needed much encouragement to offer her opinions or indeed to listen to the opinions of others and here's the proof. Hope it helps.

Dr Pete Bennett

University of Wolverhampton

Contents

Acknowledgments

Firstly, as a Christian, I am truly thankful to the Lord Jesus Christ for my gifts and allowing me to write and share my story with the world.

Writing a book is harder than I thought and more rewarding than I could have ever imagined. For many years I thought about writing a book, but I believe that timing is everything and now is the right time to share my experience. None of this would have been possible without Camelle Ilona, the ever patient, the best motivator and coach that has been on my tail every step of the way. The weekly check-ins and advice you have given me have been immeasurable. Your friendship means more to me than you will ever know.

A special thank you goes to my amazing husband, Ben, who is my biggest supporter, always offering me advice and making sure I am the best version of myself. To my boys, our sons, Gabe and Jerry, for always believing in me and allowing me to write my book and keeping out of my hair.

To my parents, Mom and Dad, without you I would not be here, and I want to say how much I appreciate you as my parents. You have always shown me the importance of working hard for what I want in life and my work ethic comes from you both. Growing up was not easy, but I know you both did your best for me, and I appreciate you.

My brothers, Daniel and Dale, the ones who got the brunt of my leadership skills as big sister, I have always demanded the best from you both and I know I can be too much, but I do love you both and want the best for you.

My amazing nephew Adam, the most creative person I know, thank you for commissioning the design my book cover and designing my logo.

Thanks to everyone who helped me make this book a reality. To my editor, Lilly, thank you for doing such an amazing job on my manuscript. To Lensi Photography, for my branding images, you are simply the best. Of course, my amazing hairdresser, Jonathan Campbell and my school friend and makeup artist, the amazing Jessica Williams.

Thanks to everyone who contributed to the book, Sandeep Laira, Charlotte Ware, Cairon Morris-Ashman, Denise Bryan-Williams, Tex Gabriel Jr, Joan Ible, Sharmain Perrin, Sabrina Dennis, Tamina Dennis, Julian Hall, Sandeep (Dr Print) Pauline (Deep Experience) and some of my Y12 students. Special thank you to, Paul Sinclair, Val Taylor and Sharmain Perrin, who read the book in its raw form and gave me some much-needed advice.

For my wonderful University lecturer, Pete Bennett, who first of all believed in me, offered me nothing but support during my university course and when I thought I could not do it and for writing my *Preface*. You are one of a kind.

A big thank you goes out to my besties, my girls who have supported me throughout this whole process and throughout some major milestones in my life. Danielle and Rebecca, I don't know where I would be without your friendship, your support, your prayers and your love. Thank you for adding value to my life and embracing my gifts.

Special thanks to my spiritual covering who happens to be my big brother and sister, Bishop Melvin and Pastor Yvonne Brooks. You both have never stopped believing in me, supporting me and keeping me accountable through all areas of my life and I'm truly blessed to have you in my life.

I would like to give a special thank you to Shirley Rolinson. You believed in me enough to employ me and allowed me to grow, even when you were questioned about your decisions. I thank you for your consistent support. To Bev Ramsell, you started as my manager and have since become my friend and someone I can count on. When I was going through a hard time, you were a listening ear and supportive friend, one I could count on, and I appreciate you. To my dear friend Lobbo Toure, you helped me to get through some of the most difficult times in my teaching career. Thank you for your positivity that carried me. You don't know how this saved my life; I appreciate your friendship.

Introduction

Isn't it funny? I have always known that there was something special about me and even though you go through life not really counting the cost of what you have been through, it wasn't until I was sat in an interview for a promotion that it occurred to me - when I was asked the question: "So tell me about yourself, how did you get here? What has brought you to this place now"?

I began telling three strangers about my life, from leaving school until the present day. After around ten minutes of hearing, they were just blown away. I remember them saying how inspired they were by my story; let alone the young people I would encounter. They highlighted my resilience, my drive and determination to achieve the very best in life. That was my lightbulb moment and it hit me; I have something to say!

I have always been drawn to young people. I think deep down, this is why I am in teaching, although when I started, I began with adults. I soon found that my love and passion was for helping young people. This led me to the point where I was going to bare all and share my story of leaving school with one GCSE grade above a 'C' (which in today's terms would have been a 5). Even though it was 27 years ago, I still remember until this day how I felt going to results day. Every year when I hear it on the news or when it comes to results day, my heart goes out to those individuals who would have tried their very best to get the grades, but for whatever reason they did not and the disappointment they would have felt. I had been there. I know what it felt like, but I also know that for me, after a day or so of crying and feeling disappointed, I got back up, planned and decided to start again in college. This was my second chance, and I took it and ran with it and now I look at myself as a graduate, as well as one who has gained invaluable experience. From lecturer, tutor, assessor and teacher, to now curriculum leader in my subject area.

Interestingly, I have experienced this as an individual, parent and teacher, so I can empathise with all parties. Grades are not the end, but the stepping stones to get you to your future destination.

Only last year, I studied for my Level 7 qualification in Careers Leadership, and this was to aid my passion to help young people find their fit in society and do something that makes them happy and fulfilled. This will be the driving force to show young people the pathways they need to take and follow their dreams.

This is why I wrote this book to inspire one young person who might be struggling and give them hope that if I can do it, they can!

Chapter 1
The Bigger Picture

It was a Wednesday afternoon (as we say, Wednesday is Hump Day), the middle of the week and I really didn't want to be at school. It was a bright clear day and we just had morning break and I was looking out the window in my English lesson. All I remember was losing it for a second, because I really was frustrated and angry. I flipped over the table in the classroom in a rage and called the teacher 'a silly cow'!!! All I knew, minutes later, I was sat outside the office of my Head of House and he was telling me that the consequences of my actions would see me excluded from school for three days. Well, I was happy to not be in school for three days, but I was dreading going home. My dad was especially strict and he would not be allowing it to be a free ride.

Fast forward three days later, taking that long walk down the school drive was like making the longest walk ever, let alone taking this walk with my parents for my return to school meeting, from being excluded. The wait for the Deputy Head was long anyway. He called us in and started to talk calmly, the next minute he was shouting at me. I remember him saying, "If you ever conduct yourself in that manner in a classroom in this school again, you will be out of here." Those words were all I needed to hear. This was a pivotal moment, one which drove me to make a decision that would literally change my life. It was peak!

So how did I get to this stage, what happened? Let me explain how I got to this point .....

From a very early age, due to a number of personal family reasons, I didn't have consistency in my education. I would be away from primary school for weeks or months at a time, which did not help me, as there were gaps in my learning. However, this was not discovered until later on, so when I started secondary school, it was a fresh start for me.

In Year 7, I was excited for the fresh start, made new friends and established myself in the school. As the year went on, I was a popular girl who had many friends. Interestingly, my friends had mixed abilities and when I was placed in my sets, to my surprise, the majority of them were in the lower sets and only a few in the higher. Most definitely I excelled in English and PE.

As most teenagers, I had an exciting first year of school and liked how different it was to primary education, so by the time I got into Year 8, I began to develop a reputation with my teachers for being a very polite but extremely chatty student. This was a consistent comment in my reports and parents evening.

The truth is, when I didn't understand something, I would just switch off and if I asked for help and didn't receive it, or time was not spent to help me to understand, I would then become disruptive in lessons. As a student who was popular, we would often have banter and jokes in lesson; it was a part of school life.

Safe to say, Years 8 and 9 were rocky years for me. I remained in the same school, but this was a mask for me, as my parents were going through a divorce which was quite volatile. I didn't know how much this affected me until I became frustrated and uncontrollable at times. I am not going to lie, I 'got shook' when I was suspended from school for flipping the table over in English (my favourite lesson); I have to be real, I was just immature. I did not like what the teacher said to me and truthfully, I was just acting out learnt behaviour from home.

Another observation which I was able to make in more recent years, was to do with my sleep. Although I had many opportunities to have an early night, I would choose to stay up later than I should have, which meant that I didn't get enough sleep. This had a major impact on my concentration in lessons, especially when I woke up tired. This would affect my mood for the most part of the morning and sometimes the entire day. As if that wasn't enough, at that time in my life, I wasn't eating breakfast consistently; my diet consisted of chocolates and other foods not great for me, a lot of chips, pizzas and burgers.

My parents were not happy I was suspended and I remember going in for my return to school meeting with the Deputy Head, who was a stern man. I mean, the man spoke so direct to me and told me if I messed up like this again, I would be out (meaning permanently excluded). If I am honest, the thing that shocked me the most was the way he spoke to me and my parents said nothing. I was looking for them to defend me, but the fact was, I was wrong.

Year 9 going into Year 10 saw a series of poor reports, not great parents' evenings and a mixture of poor choices of friendship groups. This was coupled with girls' drama, which is heightened at this age. There was one major incident that involved a group of immature boys and girls and myself and the consequence of this caused me to lose some friends. I decided it was time to fix up, no longer seeking to be the popular girl; this was hard for me as I had a lot of friends. Well, that's what I thought, but the reality was, most of them were doing a lot better at school than me, yet I was the one suffering educationally. I had that lightbulb moment and decided to start focusing on getting my head down to study for my GCSEs.

I mean those next two years were crucial!!!

The truth is, when we start out in school, we are not focused and not looking at 'the bigger picture'. I mean, we are four years old and all that is important at the time is making friends. As we progress through primary school, this continues, and we are obviously learning along the way.

Then comes the time to move to secondary school (big school). This time it's different as most things we know about school changes. We have more lessons and this time we have to move to a different classroom in between lessons. The learning gets a little harder, we are older so now have to take on more responsibility. We start developing as a teenager with hormones running rife. Making new friends is still our focus, being popular is important and ultimately, we have different priorities. This is normal. Studies have shown that young people at this stage in life have life events that don't make much sense, but it is all a part of life and we all go through it, so there is some grace here. In addition, young people have more distractions now than I did back then. Mobile phones, social media, gaming, all contribute to distractions within the mind of young people and they tend to stay up late for all of these reasons, which also impacts on their day-to-day school life.

But when does it click that we will leave this institution and be responsible to develop our own careers? The bigger picture is looking at where will I be in five, ten and fifteen years. How will I get there? What is the journey I will take to get to my final destination? All these questions are important in order for us to have some direction for the future.

Our attitude and character are also key elements to the bigger picture, because how we are now, will determine what we will be like in the future; our actions often follow us whether we like it or not. Bad reputation sticks and can also follow us, depending on the route we take, so we have to be conscious that this can impact us in the future.

Finally, I get it. Outside of school, we all have sorts of things going on; home can be a complex place for some of us. Figures from the Office for National Statistics disclose that **half of all children come from separated households and a quarter of families are headed by a single parent.** For such children, that brings all kinds of challenges and dynamics, but again another truth is, as children, the focus should be going to school to learn and gain an education that will help later in life. Instead, they are focused on what is going on at home. Sadly, this is one of the major distractions and disruptions to a young person's education. Broken homes may bring about stress, tension, lack of motivation and frustration. Obviously, these manifestations **may impact negatively on a pupil's academic performance**. Johnson, as cited in *"Influence on broken homes in Academic Performance"* (Igbinosa, 2014), indicated that children of unmarried parents or separated families often fail and are at risk emotionally. [1]

Another major factor in school were teachers. Listen, let's be real. They were like marmite; you either loved them or hated them, simple as that! And now that I am a teacher, I get it from both perspectives. I get it that teachers are under a huge amount of pressure not only to teach and impart knowledge to students, but everything else that comes with it; marking – planning – assessment and making sure all classes learn what's in the curriculum so they can pass their exams. It should not be this way but it is - that's a part of the system. As a pupil, there were some teachers who were just likeable, they developed a rapport with their pupils, down to earth and relatable and had boundaries with their students in the classroom, which meant they each respected the other. This is the kind of teacher I believe I am, as I have found my students are more engaged and motivated in lessons when they have a rapport with you. Needless to say, those teachers who were uptight, always angry, bad coffee breath (sorry not sorry LOL) they got the opposite response from me. I would very rarely approach them for help or everything else and I could not wait to get out of their lesson as soon as I got in - let's be real!

What is of particular importance is the fact that because we spend a lot of our time in school, good relationships are important and help us to flourish. I never thought I would become a teacher, as I could count on my hands the teachers I got on with and it's the teachers I liked who have made a lasting impression on me. I remember them now, thirty years plus.

---

1. https://project4topics.com/influence-of-broken-home-on-academic-performance-among-primary-school-pupils-2/

Chapter 2
It's never too late!

I remember like it was yesterday, that day I had to choose my GCSE options; if I am really honest, I feel let down by the system, why do I say this? I had a real passion for ICT, I didn't know what I wanted to do but wished it was an option I could have chosen, instead it was just a vocational course with no certificate or grade given. After some discussion with my parents, I had no choice but to choose Geography (as I hated History), Design Technology, and French for my language option. I really didn't care too much about science and Maths I hated it with a passion. The only subjects I actually wanted to do was Business and English.

I had all good intentions, taking notes in class. Some things I understood, some things went over my head, but I was determined to try. I even managed to get moved up two sets in Maths from the bottom set, after this I don't know what happened, but my motivation was gone. Really, the only subject

I made no effort in was Maths. I don't know if it was the room, or the fact that we never had a permanent teacher, but I would always find myself at the back of the class by the heater with my head down and I would just sleep, I mean fully sleeping and I can't recall being challenged either.

TOP TIPS

- *I encourage all students regardless of what age, to get a good night sleep, at least 8 hours, because this will set you up for the day and make sure you are ready to learn.*
- *Have a proper breakfast - this aids your ability to learn. Studies have shown that for children who eat breakfast, their ability to concentrate in lessons is enhanced.*
- *I would also encourage students to write down the things (topics) you don't understand in the lessons and ask the teacher after the class for 1-2-1 support.*

I went through Year 10, had my mocks, which weren't great and at this point just hated school and could not wait to leave. I continued to revise but had no clue - I mean, I was reading but it was not making a difference. I felt like it was not registering and I could not recall the information. I remained optimistic, but in the back of my mind just thought, *I should have started revising this earlier.* Some days were good, but other days I just felt deflated. However, I kept going and doing what everyone expected of me: *Go to school, behave myself, come home, lock up in my room and revise* and did this on repeat.

At this point, I was living with my mom, as she moved out of the family home; my parents were separated and my mom was a single parent. Since my mom was not as strict as my dad, I had more freedom to go out and so it was a priority to revise, but I used every opportunity to get out of it (lol).

My final year was exciting and I could hardly believe I nearly survived school. As the months drew closer, it became real, but I do remember my Leavers Assembly, where we took a short walk to a local church and I remember sitting there in a moment that seemed so surreal. This place I came to every day for five years was soon to be a memory. I recall I cried and cried at the end of the service so much that my head hurt. It's funny that you hate the place for at least four years and then when you're leaving you become emotional; bottom line was I developed relationships with friends, teachers, and created memories around the school. In fact, my final year was when I represented my school the most in athletics competitions and travelled around competing, I loved it, it was where I got my fulfilment and joy - a sense of pride. I had a great relationship with my P.E. teachers and at that point, my Head of House left a lasting impression on me. As I left for exam leave the reality hit, this was it. I put everything into doing my best in my exams and that's all I could do.

How times have changed. We have so many more GCSE options to choose from. Yes, the school you attend chooses what they offer, but with the national curriculum in place, there are some standard subjects on option. Some schools offer additional vocational subjects which allow you to gain a qualification from it. Again, this is very useful.

In my days (as we say) BTECs weren't even an option. I do believe that if it was, at the time, I would have done a lot better in my final results. I have to be real, I just don't think I'm academically inclined, but I do like to learn new things, so working on a subject where you could do coursework as well as a small exam would have worked for me.

Let's look at this further. I have heard some students say, 'I'm not doing this subject', or, 'I'm not revising as I'm not going to use or need this GCSE when I leave school anyway'. They might be right, because everyone's plan and route are different and determining what role you go into, informs what subjects you need. But all subjects you chose are relevant at some point in your life.

Maths and English are fundamental. I realised this once I left school and how I was restricted due to me not having my maths qualification. I definitely lost time having to re-do my maths GCSE in order to get into university and I took the exam 4 times before I passed. Little did I know I was going to become a Business teacher, so my GCSE Business came in handy after all. I always had a passion for Business and didn't think I would eventually own my own until I got older, but knew I would work in the business environment and needed to use the concepts. There are others such as Design Technology and Geography that

I have never used, meaning the content taught I haven't remembered, so I wonder if was it even useful for me.

This has got me thinking about short term and long-term memory and that how we respond to this may help us later in life. As well as learning, being aware of particular revision techniques early would have been beneficial to me. Let's face it, the content that is taught in Year 7 to Year 11 is a lot, but how we recall this information is key to how we perform in our exams.

I would like to suggest some ways I have proven to work, based on what my own children use now in school:

Revision/flash cards.

Something like this

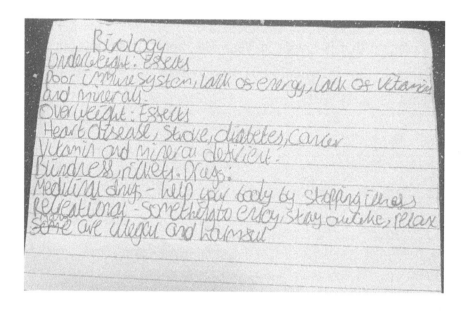

Maybe putting a key term on the front and meaning on the back, or question or heading on the front and meaning on the back

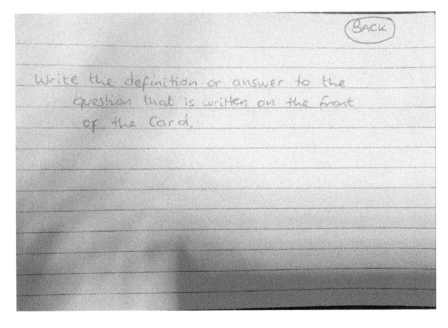

Revision checklists

You can have a subject in the middle and then sub-topics and information coming from them.[1]

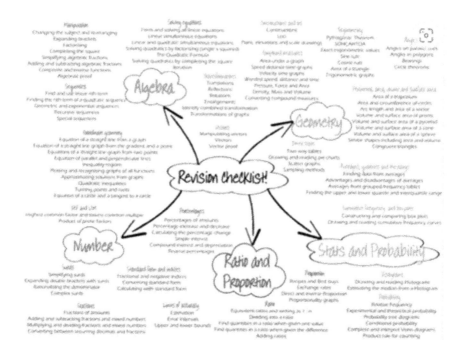

Revision clocks

Finding 12 key points from topics and answering them within the spaces given[2]

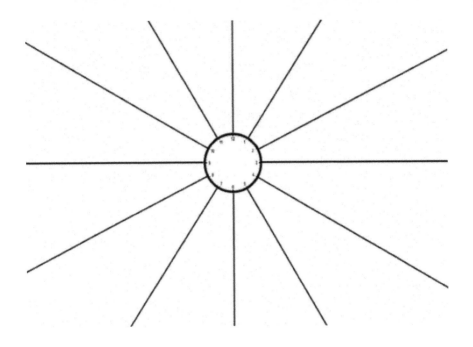

Mind Maps[3]

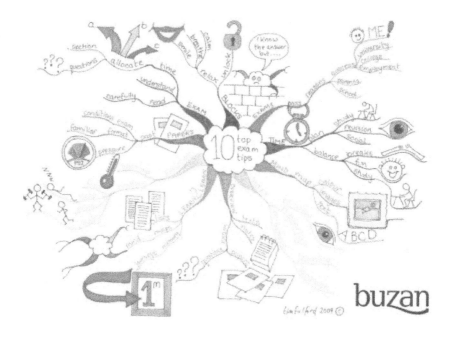

1. https://www.yumpu.com/xx/document/view/61767025/higher-revision-checklist
2. https://www.tes.com/teaching-resource/blank-revision-clock-pdf-12100296
3. Mind Maps | GCSE Maths (wordpress.com)

Chapter 3
"Show me what you've got"

In this chapter we are going to look at the importance of work experience and how it helps when we leave school, to have transferable skills which will help us in the world of work. My work experience has varied over the years where I have undertaken a number of roles. I was extremely blessed to have been offered employment in some of the companies in which I have worked.

A part of growing up is the dream of having your first job. Following your careers talks, the school will introduce opportunities for work experience. I remember my school planned for us to complete this in Year 10 and I struggled to find my own placement, but the school helped me with this, and I was offered a role at ASDA in a nearby shopping mall.

It was so exciting starting my first day at a large company and to tell the truth, so grateful I was not in school. They allowed me to work in several departments to have a good scope of the organisation. Although I loved this experience as the week went on, I was surprised to learn even in ASDA, that you needed to have good GCSEs in order to be employed by them. I enjoyed the week but realised retail was not for me.

As I began to enter into Year 11, I started to research summer holiday jobs and subsequently started with working in my church's bakery, in the factory and the office. As my parents worked in the catering industry, I was able to gain valuable experience in silver service from an early age. This led to me being successful with a job within the hotel industry as a silver service waitress. I stayed there for three years while studying in my sixth form years. Alongside this, I have worked in hotels, McDonalds, in office roles such as credit controller, administrator, all before I started to pursue a career in teaching. When I was finishing my studies of what I would focus on in teaching, in 1999, I went into a role at the bank as customer service advisor, mainly to get some money to pay for our wedding. I was in this role for three years and after I got my qualifications to start teaching, decided to hand in my notice and pursue teaching full time.

After I got married in 2002, I decided to launch my first business with a friend. For many years I had a passion for events, and I was friends with someone who had the same passion, so we decided to set up together, but each of us would specialise in our area of expertise.

For many years I desired to have a business but didn't know how and where to start. I got advice and created my business plan and as I was only 22 years old, I was able to secure some funding through 'The Princes Trust' to help with start-up costs. All of the experience I have gained and developed over the years has enabled me to do so much more in my lifetime. Never underestimate experience you have gained as this can be your stepping-stone onto the next opportunity.

This was my time to try new roles, after all I was still young, I didn't have any dependents (children) and could be more flexible with roles I had. After three years of working with the bank, I finally took the plunge to work fewer hours but at a higher hourly rate. In Further Education I could afford to do this, so I was connected with someone in a college who was able to offer me 20 hours a week teaching - this was the beginning of my journey into Education and teaching, as I wanted. My first year in teaching was good, I taught at three different sites for the college, teaching 16+ pupils in Information Technology. This is where my real test started, as my patience was tested. This was the first year and this would be the deciding factor of whether I could continue to do this.

After the year, I needed to secure something more permanent, so I applied for a role in a local Learn Direct centre as 'IT Support Tutor'. It was an interesting role and everything was done electronically - the courses, the induction and the final exams or assessments. In this role, I was able to achieve my maths qualification finally, which meant I could work towards my goal of attending university to complete my Certificate in Education, a recognised qualification to enable me to teach in colleges and schools. Needless to say, it took me nearly nine months to get my pass grade. It was challenging, but my goal was stronger, so after every fail, I continued to go for the next exam until I got my pass grade in October 2004. I was able to get into university and started the following November. It was an interesting course that taught me so much about teaching and planning. During my time on the course, I discovered I needed to get a number of teaching hours in order to pass one of the modules and because I was in a support role, I began my search to find a job where I could teach to gain my hours. After fourteen months, I left to start a role within the NHS as an 'IT Trainer'. Fast forward to July 2005, I had the proud moment of graduating from university, something I never thought would happen.

Once I graduated, there started to be some changes within the NHS and there was talk of the ECDL qualification which I was delivering, coming to an end. In addition, where I lived in comparison to where I worked, was some distance to journey every day, so I decided I was going to use the opportunity to explore different educational settings. I therefore began supply work, where I worked in Primary and Secondary schools. This for me was an eye opener, as I never thought I would like teaching in schools. I continued to gain experience and each school was different, the money was good and I had no responsibility for marking or administration, I just went to cover classes. In March 2006, I began a long-term supply role at a local school which I fell in love with; I was teaching in secondary schools and had so much fun interacting with the young people. I did this role for nine months and then decided I wanted to gain a full degree so I would have no barriers to me teaching full time or permanently in schools.

I went through the university application, received an offer, secured a part time job in Events to support me alongside studying again. I didn't have children so could afford to do this. However, in the back of my mind, I was still desiring to work full time in a Further Education college again, so was still applying for roles when they came up. This particular summer, I had two interviews, one as a 'Functional Skills tutor', the other as 'Trainer Assessor in IT'. I was successful with the 'Trainer Assessor' role, so had to make the hard decision to turn down the university offer, leave my new part time role and start my new career in this college, where in fact I worked for twelve years. During that period, I undertook so much personal development that I was able to complete my Level 5 management course, my BA Hons Degree in conjunction with University of Wolverhampton and numerous other courses. All this was done at no cost to me as my employer had agreements and covered the costs. These were now added to my other qualifications such as Microsoft Office Specialist, Functional Skills, Maths, English and ICT, Health and Safety qualifications, to name a few.

After twelve years, I could see no room for progression for me in the organisation. I always saw myself in management, but whenever an opportunity would come up, I would apply, but there was either someone already earmarked for the job role, or the feedback was that I was lacking something, which negatively affected my score. This happened on three separate occasions with management roles. I felt like as a black woman within an organisation, that I was not valued for what I could bring to the roles and that my voice was not being heard. During my final year at the college, I experienced bullying from a senior manager who was unhappy that I had been successful in securing a management role as 'Learning and Development coach'. It was then that I decided it was time for me to return to secondary schools. Unfortunately, I was forced out of my job and my mental health at this point was under attack and so I left.

I started off working in a newly established Alternative Provision school in Walsall, again, a challenging but great role where I enjoyed working. Sadly, it was only three afternoons a week so after eight months this was not sustainable, prompting me to start my job search again. This time I secured a teaching role within a school, teaching Business.

I did this role six months prior to the pandemic, working through this period, as well as after. I then felt the push to pursue even more earnestly, so started looking for Head of Department roles. Subsequently, I was offered a job as 'Curriculum Leader for Businesses' at a newly opened school within Birmingham. This role was perfect for me, and I worked with some amazing staff and students, but unfortunately, after six months into the role, I was told they were making my role redundant, as they didn't have the numbers for the course they had expected. Needless to say, this was an emotional time for me, one I never expected to happen.

So now my journey shifted course, with me teaching part-time at a school and on the look-out for another 'Head of Business' role coming up at a school.

This experience over the years has benefited me in the sense that I have worked for several different types of employers and organisations and the different settings allowed me to see things from different perspectives.

I had great experiences in some work settings, such as building relationships with staff and teachers who remain friends until this day and the experience of teaching different subjects was always going to be a bonus to my career. I would take on extra responsibilities to help the schools, but I also experienced some really challenging ones, all of which have helped to build my character and resilience and showed me where I needed to be. I have experienced bullying on the job, injustice in regard to things that have happened to me mostly from senior leaders in these organisations, so I felt like I never had a voice to be able to speak up. Especially as a black woman, I always felt like it was so much harder for me to progress as people had fears and doubts about black people in leadership. I never regret the experiences I have had, as in every experience it has taught me something about others and about myself.

Practical Tips

1. *In every organisation you work in, try and gain some skills to help you in the next role*
2. *If you have access to free CPD, personal or professional development, take it; it will help you to secure different opportunities later*
3. *When applying for roles always consider your commute and if you know you cannot keep it up don't accept it.*

Chapter 4
Results Day

Results day, a day I remember so well. At the time, the pressure I felt was huge and living in a single parent home where my mom had to work, I found myself going to collect my results alone. My mom was at work and due to the breakup, had a strained relationship with my dad who was also at work that day. I remember getting on the 51 bus to take what I thought was the longest journey ever, from Lozells to Great Barr and as I did on a daily basis, took that walk down Wilderness Lane to go into school to collect my results from the school hall. If I am honest to myself, I didn't know how I did and never expected to open the envelope and see one subject with a grade of B/C. All the others were below C, so D, E, F (in today's equivalent it would be 3, 2 and 1; and, of course with Maths, a U grade (ungraded). I tried. I never expected a Fail, but I remember having a brief conversation with a teacher and then, to be frank, I left, speechless.

The room was buzzing with so many emotions - people happy, crying, happy/sad tears. Some people seemed confused, but I remember thinking, *just get me out of here!* I remember going home and being upset as family and friends called to find out what results I got. I remember saying I passed, because technically, if you got any grade, it was a Pass, but as you can imagine they wanted to know what grades I got. That's where it got tricky and I then had to explain myself. I could sense the disappointment and concern, but what could I do as I couldn't change anything.

I remember that evening I reflected on what I had achieved. I mean, my whole school life (five years) and I left with one decent grade above C, I mean. *I messed up!* That's all I could think, and I cried myself to sleep as I felt like I disappointed myself and everyone else.

The next day I continued to plan to enrol on an apprenticeship scheme in a Sixth Form college, doing business administration, which I loved. The structure of the college week appealed as I only had four days at college and one day release. I remember this college was where some of my close friends already attended, they were a year older than me, but I felt happy as I knew people there.

That summer I got my first summer job, working for my church's bakery. Unfortunately, due to my poor results this was all I could get and I was recommended to work here by a friend. It was very low wages, but it was enough for me to get by as I lived at home and it gave me the opportunity to work out what would happen next.

PRACTICAL TIPS

- *Remember results day is not the end. Yes, people will be disappointed, but it does not define you.*
- *Make sure you seek careers advice and guidance to help you map out your next steps in order to reach your goal.*

I conducted a survey and spoke to different people who would have a vested interest in exam results, I asked them a series of questions, and these are the results.

Teachers:

The morning of results day, how do you feel?

At the end of results day, how do you feel?

How important is results day to you? And what is the impact?

Sandeep Laira

I felt quite nervous for the students because I knew how hard they had worked and as it was the first year after the pandemic, I was concerned for how the grade boundaries would work.

When I knew how they had performed after data sent via colleagues, I felt relieved that they had done so well, disappointed for the ones that missed out by a few marks.

I think it's an important day for staff and students, we want to know what worked for which students and who truly put the work in to see how well they did.

Cairon Morris-Ashman

The week leading up to results day causes me palpitations each year, especially for my Year 13 pupils. The day before, I get little or no sleep. I panic about possible questions that may trip the kids up.

At the end of results day, thankfully they've mostly been positive, I feel relief, satisfaction that my pupils' hard work has paid off.

I think it's more important for the pupils than for me, but I get a sense of validation for the efficiency of my planning and delivery to impact pupils' grades. It is a reaffirmation of why I tolerate the marginalisation, the rude demands from parents and blatant disregard from some pupils.

Charlotte Ware

I tend to start feeling nervous/anxious for results day around a week before and as the day comes closer, this feeling increases. I do also tend to wake in the night thinking about it.

I know deep down I have done all I could have over the past two years to support the students, but I can't help but torture myself thinking, was there anything else!

I don't really feel an importance for myself towards results day, I feel the importance for the students. I know that these results can shape their journey moving forward and I just want students to have done the best they possibly could, I can't help but feel disappointment and upset when I see that some students may not have achieved as well as they should have or had hoped.

Denise Bryan-Williams

I would feel nervous and hopeful for the students but incredibly nervous as the teacher. Had I done a good enough job? Had they remembered everything? Had I met my own performance management target?

At the end of the results day, mostly relieved. Happy for the students, heartbroken for others even if they hadn't worked hard enough.

It was never the most important day of the year. There is so much more to education and the pupils' overall development, that this one day held more significance than it should have. Even a bad set of results can be turned around.

It can leave some pupils feeling like failures although for many it is an exciting way to end their time at school. The end of lots of hard work. Very difficult, though, for pupils that have always struggled. Never liked results day for many of them.

Y12 student:

The morning of results day how did you feel?

After you received your results how did you feel?

Did you have any regrets?

Did the results you received cause any barriers for you? If so explain

Tamina Dennis

The morning of results day: I felt extremely nervous but, at the same time I was excited because I knew I was stepping into a new chapter. However, I was also scared because I knew that if I didn't get the grades I wanted, I wouldn't be able to get into my chosen sixth form.

After I received my results: I felt a huge relief, however, I was very upset because as I was given predicted grades, they weren't as high as they should have been and I felt as though it wasn't my best. I knew I could've achieved greater.

I don't have many regrets. The only regret I would say I had was not asking for help sooner when I needed it. However, I thoroughly enjoyed secondary school and made amazing memories! Would do anything to go back.

Yes, I wasn't allowed to take sociology at A level due to my maths grade, so this prevented me from being able to do that course. However, I'm currently still doing three A level subjects that I enjoy so it didn't turn out that bad!

A Group of Students – results:

1. The morning of results day how did you feel?

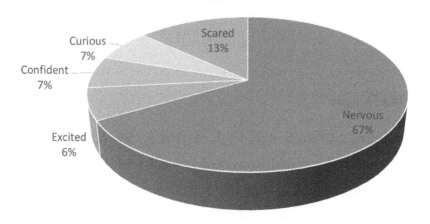

2. After you received the results how did you feel?

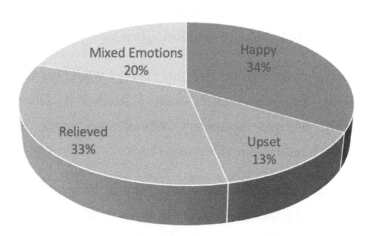

3. Did you have any regrets?

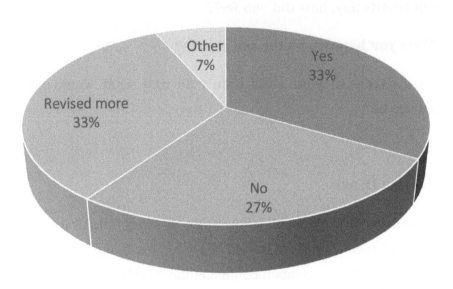

4. Did the results you received cause any barriers for you?

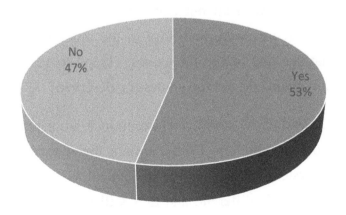

Parent:

On results day, how did you feel?

Were you happy with the end results?

As a parent, if your child didn't do well what would your advice be?

Sabrina Dennis

I had nervous excitement; it was a very difficult time as we were in the pandemic, and we couldn't be sure how things were being done. There was so much confusion the year before, so we just held on to the fact that we knew she had tried her best and that her mock grades were good, so we should be okay. But it wasn't easy to stay positive given the circumstances.

We were happy with all but one result that needed to be re-marked, the scores were not close to the mock or class work marks that she had before the exams. Happy to say once they looked at it again, she got the grades she deserved.

It's not the end of the world, we have to look at the reasons why and support our children. Exams are not for everyone, and the education system is based on one size fits all, however we know that every child is different, and they will progress in different ways. We can retake exams and move on to the next thing. The most important thing is to offer support and be there for them.

Sharmain Perrin

Nervous, concerned that if my son didn't get the results he deserved, that he would have been devastated.

He did amazingly so there was no need for worry.

Don't be defined nor deterred by it. Press on for what you want because you can do it!

Joan Ible

I was overjoyed that my son was afforded the opportunity to sit his exams.

The results were the best that he could have done, and I was a very happy parent.

If he didn't do as well as he should have, the first thing I would have done is reassure him that it was okay. Then get him to review and assess how he feels. Based on that, we could look at a plan on moving forward, always encouraging. Every child is unique.

Employer:

As an employer how important are results when deciding who to employ?

When employing someone, is there any qualification you look for and why?

Would their grades stop you from employing someone?

Employer 1 - Pauline Walters (Deep Caribbean Experience)

As an employer, it is important to aim to select the right employee for the job, to ensure the efficiency, productivity and excellent reputation of the business are maintained.

As my business is within the hospitality sector, the qualification I would look for is basic hygiene and food handling, practical kitchen skills and good customer service, because these are the basic skills I would require as a starting point to develop self-confidence, with future practical training.

Although grades are a very important factor in today's world, it would not stop me from employing someone, as long they are willing to learn, able to adapt to changes, have good communication skills and can work well within the team.

I left school with no qualifications, however I was willing to learn and develop, so I worked hard to achieve my goals. At the age of 56, I decided I would like to learn more about the business side of my industry and embarked on a 4-year full-time University course, which was very challenging, especially at my age (which did not hinder me to achieve excellence) and running a business full-time, but my hard work and dedication paid off. At the end of the four years, I graduated at 60 and achieved a Bachelor of Honours 2-1 Degree, which has helped me to fulfil my dream of running my own business.

So, my message is as long as you apply yourself, work hard and focus on the finish line you can achieve whatever you put your mind to.

Employer 2 - Sandeep (Dr Print)

Results provide an overview of academic ability. However, I've been in business for 16 years and appreciate that grades do not paint the complete picture. In my merchandise business, good English and Maths are what to look for when we screen candidates, because having the ability to communicate clearly (both in writing and verbally) is essential, as well as numeracy to provide accurate quotes.

Conversely, we have employed candidates with low academic ability but have shown qualities like confidence, reasoning and problem solving. If a candidate has other employable qualities such as these, and they show willingness to improve on academic skills required for a role, then we would consider employing them.

The qualification would depend on the role for which we were recruiting. In our print and merchandising business, we value industry experience more than qualifications. For example, if we were recruiting for a sales role, we are more likely to employ candidates that have worked in our trade, and experience would have more weight than qualifications. However, for a marketing role, we would consider qualifications and experience.

Grades would not necessarily stop me from employing someone. As mentioned above, in most cases we would look at experience first. However, if the role requires a certain level of academic qualifications, we would have looked at both grades and experience.

Entrepreneur:

How have your grades impacted on your entrepreneurial journey?

What advice would you give a school leaver about their results?

Would grades stop you from employing someone and why?

Tex. Gabriel Jnr

Grades have not impacted my entrepreneurial journey. I learned much more from doing stuff than things I've learned in education.

Going into Higher Education was a good place to network, meet people and grow up a bit, so get the results you need to study the areas you are interested in.

My advice to school leavers about results is that it may seem like the most important thing in the world right now, but in 20 years' time it probably won't have had much effect on your life. Knowledge is good. Learn how to learn. The grades you get on a particular test are just a snapshot of how well you know that subject at that time. Keep it in perspective.

Grades would not stop me from employing someone. Character is more important than grades. You can teach what needs to be done, you can't teach honesty, hard work, and punctuality.

Obviously if you want to be a doctor you need to know how to do certain things before training, so it's all relative.

Julian Hall

As a successful entrepreneur, I can say with confidence that school grades have not had a negative impact on my entrepreneurial journey. While good grades may open doors to certain opportunities, they are by no means the only path to success.

In fact, as an entrepreneur, I have found that traits such as creativity, resilience, adaptability, and the ability to take calculated risks are far more important than a perfect academic record. These are the qualities that help entrepreneurs overcome challenges, identify new opportunities, and turn their visions into reality.

To school leavers, I would advise that while good grades are certainly something to be proud of, they are not the be-all and end-all. Regardless of your exam results, it is important to continue to develop skills, learn from experience, and seek out new opportunities. If you have good grades, congratulations, but don't let them become a crutch or an excuse for complacency. If you didn't get the grades you wanted, don't despair. There are many successful entrepreneurs who didn't do well in school but went on to achieve great things.

As an entrepreneur and employer, I believe that grades are just one factor to consider when evaluating a potential hire. While academic achievements may be important for certain roles, such as those that require specific technical or scientific knowledge, they are not necessarily indicative of a person's overall capabilities, work ethic, or potential for success.

I would be more interested in a candidate's experience, their drive, their creativity, and their ability to work well in a team. A willingness to learn and adapt is also critical, as the world of business is constantly evolving and changing.

In short, while good grades may be a helpful asset, they are not essential for success in the entrepreneurial world. Focus on developing your skills, pursuing your passions, and embracing new challenges, and you will find that opportunities will present themselves, regardless of your exam results.

Chapter 5
Fresh Start

Freedom was all that was ringing in my ears, it seemed 'long' when I was at school, I was told what to do and now my education was finally in my hands. Going to a local Sixth Form College, doing a hands-on apprenticeship course which allowed me to have a day release in a work placement, this was perfect for me.

At this college some of my long-time friends attended so I didn't feel alone. In fact, I felt responsible for where I would go and suddenly, I felt all grown up. Enrolment day was the start for me; it was exciting. I was starting a new educational experience and it was a chance for me to prove I could do this.

I loved that we didn't start college until 2 weeks into September, so I had some time at home to chill and my timetable for college was flexible. This meant I didn't need to go in all day - some lessons were in the morning, some started in the afternoon.

There was something different about college. My motivation was different so I wanted to be there; the subject, the course content was one of my passions, so it was easy for me to engage and understand. What was great for me was getting a taste of working life, as one day a week I spent the day in an office. It opened my eyes into how working in an office would be.

The thing that stuck me the most about college was that if I decided I wasn't going to come into college because it was cold or if I was too tired, no one really followed up. It seemed like it wasn't an issue, not like when I was at school. I would always call in to explain where I was and when I came into college the next day, the lecturer would ask where I was, but it just didn't seem like a big deal.

My year went quickly I had a positive year and experience, being able to study NVQ Level 1 and Level 2 in a year was great. My only regret was that I did not retake my GCSE Maths, although I did Key Skills, but I did not complete the course. I just hated Maths and felt like I could get on without it. As the end of the academic year approached, I asked my lecturer if I could continue to the next level up for the qualification I was doing, but unfortunately, the college was not running this course.

Basically, I was in control of my education from this point on. If I didn't attend, that was on me and it would be my responsibility to catch up. Thankfully, the course I was doing was based on practical coursework, so I had to make sure my work was completed by a deadline date in order to pass my qualification. Now, I had to start again and search for a local college which would deliver my course at Level 3. However, no college did, so in a last-minute panic, I enrolled onto the GCSE Law course at a college 10 minutes away from my first college. I was devastated not to be continuing in the same college as my friends. This time I literally knew no one, so I came in only to attend my classes and then left.

Now, I felt like I was back to rock bottom, where I knew no one and I was studying a course I had no interest in and no motivation to complete. It was time for me to make a decision. I was in Year 13 and had no clue what I was going to do next. This year was finally coming to an end and somehow, I sat the exam and achieved a 'D' grade (Grade 3). I had some real decisions to make with regard to what was I going to do next, particularly bearing in mind that I had a bad experience within my primary education. At the age of 17, I had a feeling that I would like to teach but never thought I would teach in a school, but I began to research my possibilities of teaching in a Further Education College.

Remember I said earlier, that in school I had a passion for ICT and now there were real ICT qualifications that I could achieve, which would allow me to do what I loved. I had a flashback to when I was growing up and how I always used to teach my teddy bears. Then I remember someone saying to me, 'You usually have an idea what career you will do by what you used to do in play as a child.' This for me was simple. I taught, worked in an office and was a natural leader.

Just when I approached 18 years, I finally decided to study for some IT qualification for a year with a view to teaching this eventually. YES!!! I felt like I was finally getting back on track, and I had a goal and focus for where I was going. I was back on the right track and the right course, and it felt good. The setbacks didn't stop me but finally helped me to discover my destiny after two years of leaving school.

I would now like to have a deeper look into possible Further Education routes once you leave school. There are many options, as not everyone will do the same thing, so let's explore some possible routes:

Apprenticeships

An apprenticeship is a paid job where the employee learns and gains valuable experiences. Alongside on-the-job training, apprentices spend at least twenty per cent of their working hours completing classroom-based learning with a college, university or training provider which leads to a nationally recognised qualification.[1]

There are four types of apprenticeships in the UK: Immediate, Advance, Higher and Degree.

An apprenticeship is a real job where you learn, gain experience and get paid. You're an employee with a contract of employment and holiday leave. By the end of an apprenticeship, you'll have the right skills and knowledge needed for your chosen career.

For more information on apprenticeships visit:

www.apprenticeships.gov.uk

Further Education College

- GCSE retakes in English and Maths and some offer A levels.
- Vocational subjects - these are related to a broad subject area such as business, health and social care, etc. - so they can lead to a large variety of employment areas or university courses.
- Practical Vocational courses that lead to specific jobs such as hairdressing, plumbing, or engineering.
- T Levels - new 2-year job-related qualifications equivalent to three A Levels.
- Apprenticeships - where a student is mostly based with a paying employer and is assessed either in that workplace by a visiting assessor or by attending a college for a day or week at a time.
- Courses that prepare people for Higher Education, such as Access Courses or the Art Foundation/Post - A level Art Course
- Vocational Higher Education Level courses, such as Foundation Degrees, Higher National Diplomas (HNDs) and Certificates (HNCs)
- Foundation Courses to develop Maths, English, study skills, confidence and employability. These courses can give students the chance to try out several different vocational areas.

- Learning for leisure - these courses are usually part-time and often in the evenings. They may involve learning more about a hobby or interest e.g. ceramics, art.
- Courses aimed at overseas students - such as English Language Courses or preparation courses for university.

All young people must now stay in education or training until their 18th birthday and many young people choose to go to Further Education College so they can develop their skills and qualifications before they progress into a job or higher education course, either at a college or a university.

For further information on why you might choose to go to college visit:

www.careerpilot.org.uk[2]

Employment

Employment most generally means the state of having a paid job, of being employed. To employ someone is to pay them to work. An employer provides employment to employees. Employment can also refer to the act of employing people, as in "We're working to increase our employment of women". [3]

5 main types of employment are:[4]

- Full-time and part-time employees.
- Casual employees.
- Fixed term and contract employees.
- Apprentices and trainees.
- Commission and piece rate employees.

Entrepreneur

There are a number of reasons why someone would want to be an entrepreneur. They often get into entrepreneurship because they question the status quo and wonder if there might be a better way to do things. They may also identify a gap in services, knowledge, or support in their community and decide to address it with a great business idea or an unconventional solution.[56]

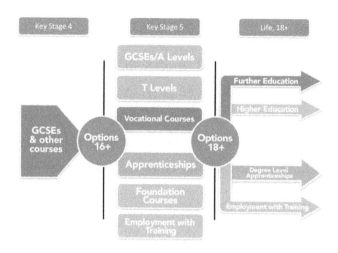

PRACTICAL TIPS

- *Make sure you do your research before leaving education to have a 2-year course for Y12 and Y13*
- *Make sure you follow your dream and don't do a course because of wanting to stay at a particular location or because of friends doing a course. You need to do a course that is going to get you somewhere at the end of it.*
- *You are in control of your destiny, be resilient!*

---

1. https://www.apprenticeships.gov.uk/influencers/what-is-an-apprenticeship#
2. https://www.careerpilot.org.uk/information/further-education-at-16/eleven-reasons-to-choose-an-fe-college-course
3. https://www.dictionary.com/browse/employment
4. https://www.smallbusiness.wa.gov.au/people/types-employment
5. https://www.ownr.co/blog/why-become-an-entrepreneur/
6. https://images.app.goo.gl/yz3SvkyU2p15uFNBA

Chapter 6
What is your learning style?

After a year of studying for my IT qualifications, I began a relationship. We had made plans to get married in a year, so I made a decision to go into full time work so I could save to pay for the wedding. I always had in the back of my mind that I would return to study for my teaching qualification, but for now, I was focused on having the best wedding ever!

Fast forward six months after our wedding and I was ready to continue my studies as well as working full time. I enrolled on an adult education teacher training course stage 1. This was hard, but I was focused and determined to complete it. As I began this course, we started to explore and learn about different learning styles. This was a new concept to me, but as I began to discover the pedagogy of learning, it all started to make sense.

Did you know?

We have 3 main types of learning styles:

- Visual
- Auditory
- Kinestetic

There are others as well, but we generally tend to focus on these three. One of the things I had to do, is to work out what our learning style was. Again, it was an eye-opener. When I discovered my learning styles were

VISUAL & KINESTETIC

All of my learning experience (especially secondary school) started to flash before me, *Oh that's why I struggled in this lesson,* because it was the teacher talking at me and I was not learning anything. However, the lessons where I could do practical tasks (such as P.E. and drama), I loved.

There are four predominant learning styles: Visual, Auditory, Read/Write, and Kinaesthetic. While most of us may have some general idea about how we learn best, often it comes as a surprise when we discover what our predominant learning style is.

Peter Honey and Alan Mumford developed the Learning Styles Theory -- a follow up to the work of David Kolb and his Experiential Learning Theory. Honey and Mumford identified four different styles of learning: "activist," "theorist", "reflector" and "pragmatist." According to the theory, different people naturally gravitate toward a particular learning style. Therefore, to achieve optimum learning, Honey and Mumford argue that one must identify his natural learning style, understand it and find ways to learn that complement the style.[1]

Activist

Activists are "doers" and "go-getters." They need to take action, get involved and fully immerse themselves in a learning situation. Activists are open-minded when it comes to learning, too. They are willing to try new things without pre-judgement. They approach new tasks with eagerness and excel in high-pressure situations. Learning activities most suited to activists include teamwork, role-play and participating in competitions. Activists thrive when working with people and when there is drama and a new challenge at hand.

Theorist

Theorists tend to think carefully and logically about situations, preferring to work within a given system or model. They do not allow their emotions to affect the conclusions they make when learning and instead, question everything. They do not make assumptions without undertaking thorough research and analysis. Theorists shy away from creativity and prefer to work in logical and practical terms, basing their learning on established concepts, theories and methods. Theorists respond well to learning activities that enable them to use statistics, compile evidence and ask questions.

Reflector

Reflectors like to take a step back from a situation and learn by observation, rather than jumping into action and making snap decisions. Instead of getting actively involved in a discussion or event, reflectors tend to sit back, listen, look at things from different perspectives and then take some time to mull things over before coming to a conclusion. Reflectors learn best through questionnaires, interviews, feedback and observational activities. They prefer to take part in activities that allow them to think before acting, undertake research and watch events unfold from the side-lines.

Pragmatists

Pragmatists prefer to apply knowledge and theories in a practical and literal sense and to the world around them. They learn by testing and experimenting ideas and solving problems. They prefer not to take part in discussions about how theories work. Instead, they like to put things into action. Pragmatists respond well to learning that can be directly and easily applied to the world around them. They welcome the opportunity to experiment and apply what they have learned in a practical way.

Peter Honey and Alan Mumford recommend that to maximise personal learning, each learner ought to understand their own learning style and seek out opportunities to learn in their learning style. But they should also develop their learning capacity in other styles to become a more well-rounded learner.[2]

Determining students' learning styles provides information about their specific preferences. Understanding learning styles can make it easier to create, modify, and develop more efficient curriculum and educational programs. [3]

PERSONAL BENEFITS

- *Increases your self-confidence.*
- *Improves your self-image.*
- *Teaches you how to best use your brain.*
- *Gives insight into your strengths, weaknesses, and habits.*
- *Enables you to enjoy any learning process.*
- *Inspires greater curiosity and motivation for lifelong learning.*

---

1. Honey and Mumford Learning Styles Explained (expertprogram-management.com)
2. https://extensionaus.com.au/extension-practice/peter-honey-and-alan-mumford-learning-styles/
3. https://bmcmededuc.biomedcentral.com/articles/10.1186/s12909-018-1400-2

Chapter 7
Uni not for me!

Have you ever been asked that famous question: "What do you want to be when you are older?"

A question often asked at various times in your life, you know when you are 7or 8 years old, and your auntie and uncle ask you this. Our first response would be something exciting, something we were good at, or something that interested us. As we got into Year 9, we started to spend more time considering careers. Was it because we were about to choose our GCSE options, or was it due to the fact that in three years all the work we had done would be working towards an end goal or career?

I knew that I had a passion for computers and IT, and I was an organised, administrative person, so I saw myself working in an office. As time went by, I started to discover no real career opportunities for me in computing or ICT as there was no GCSE in this subject. The school just offered it as a vocational option and there was no formal qualification. My career options became limited. There was nothing else I could see myself doing and nothing I was passionate about. I felt like the system let me down, so some of the GCSE options I chose were simply because there was no choice - that was it.

Based on my experience of school and education, my career focus became exploring apprenticeships. I just wanted to do something less academic and more practical and the idea of earning some money at the same time was appealing to me. So as the time to finish school began to draw closer, I decided to do a qualification in administration with a one-day (day release) to work in an office. I felt it was a great balance for me, and I would make the most of it. One thing I knew for sure and wasn't afraid to say, was that university just wasn't for me. I had seen friends go off to university and come home after three years with thousands of pounds of debt and a struggle to get a job related to the degree they had just studied for. To me this was a waste of time and resources. I get that some of them used it as an opportunity to leave home and experience living independently, but why all the expense!!! I just didn't get it.

My reservations for going to university personally, was that I never felt I was good enough to go. I mean, I must be honest, I was not the brightest student and the thought of having to sit in hours and hours of lectures put me right off! LOL especially as my learning style is NOT auditory.

Fast forward to 1998 when I first decided I wanted to be a teacher, a mentor told me that if I was teaching in adult education, I wouldn't need a degree. Great, I thought, having an increase in pay and doing what I love made sense and I didn't need to go to university but little did I know this was just the beginning of my teaching career.

Moving quickly on to 2002, I came out of education for a few years to save money for my wedding and then a year after I got married decided to work full time and pursue my teacher training qualifications, which I did in the evenings. It was hard work, but as I completed one stage of Adult Education Teacher Training, I wanted to do the next stage. I remember after completing my stage 2, meeting someone who told me that in order to obtain a Certification in Education which was equivalent to a teaching degree, I only had to study one year. I thought great, this would give me the chance to work in schools and colleges and earn more money.

On my enrolment day, I realised my first barrier was not getting all my GCSE qualification, as I was told that I needed a 'C' grade or above in Maths and English, but I needed to work towards getting Maths. The GCSE Maths content was irrelevant to me as I did not connect with it and felt it was useless as I did not use in everyday life. Therefore, I explored other options such as functional skills qualification which would allow me to gain an equivalent to 'C' if I gained/passed level 2. So, I began. It was no surprise that it took me a whole year to achieve this grade and on my 4th exam, I passed, giving me the Certificate I needed to finally enrol at my local university. This was big for me, but now that I had a goal in mind, I had a career objective. Going to university would give me further prospects to consider, not forgetting I had my own home and was married, so I didn't have any added expenses apart from a £5,000 loan I took to help with a computer and books.

That November in 2004 was a turning point for me, but I studied for a year with amazing supportive lecturers who helped to draw out of me what I thought I could not achieve, and I passed and had my first graduation in 2005, "Certificate in Education", what a day that was! After the graduation, I made a decision that I wanted a change, as I was an IT Trainer in the public sector and really didn't enjoy my job, so I handed in my notice and decided to finally go against my misconception of secondary school and become a supply teacher. The money was good, I was on flexible learning for around 5 months, until I was given a long-term supply role teaching IT in a local school.

Well safe to say, I absolutely loved my experience at this school. The staff were lovely and the pupils too. I really connected with the pupils who were aged 11-16 and the next 5 months was an eye opener. I remember as the weeks started to approach the end of school term, the Head of Department had a conversation with me. His words to me were, 'We have really enjoyed having you here and I would have offered you a job, if you had a degree.' I kinda knew this day was coming, so over the summer I had some thinking to do. I just didn't want to continue in different schools. I was so settled in this one and my experience was good. I spoke to my husband and decided I was finally going to enrol to complete my IT degree and work part time to help contribute to the household finances. My plan was set. I secured an unconditional offer and a part time job in another university doing a role which was another passion of minor events!

I began working there towards the end of the summer. In the meantime, I was still applying for local Further Education (FE) colleges for full time roles, as I had been applying for jobs for nearly a year and no joy! So, guess what? After 2 weeks of working in my part time role, I was offered an interview at a college not far away. I always knew that once I got into a good FE college, I would be able to progress. At this stage, I desired to be in leadership and management and so I made this known at my interview. I was offered the job the same day and again hit another crossroad.

Is the concept of having a 'career' over for good? (ibtimes.co.uk)[1]

I slept on it and had conversations with my husband but decided not to turn down this opportunity to work for a Further Education college, as I believed it would just open more doors. I left the part time job and withdrew from the university course to pursue a career as Trainer Assessor – IT, something I had not done before, but knew I wanted to learn, and I wanted change.

It's funny how good things seem to happen all at the same time. The first week I started my new job, my husband and I closed on the purchase of our first home. It was all such a new and exciting time. I remember wanting to own this home and pursuing until we eventually did, it wasn't easy as the deposit we had to find was big, but it came to pass in the end.

Only after being in the job for 6 weeks, I found out I was pregnant with our first child, something we were shocked and excited about. If I am honest, I was so afraid to tell my manager as I had just started the job. Now I was going to have to be off on maternity leave.

Some months later, I went on maternity leave for 12 months and returned to work to more change. The manager who had interviewed me was a complete 'angel' in my first year at the college and had left the college due to ill health, but before she left, organised for me to be enrolled as part of staff development, on the CMI Level 5 Leadership & Management Diploma. I mean, I've had no formal experience of managing, other than in the voluntary sector and I was able to put my skills into practice and gain a qualification to enhance this.

While on this course, one of the lecturers who was a fellow colleague spoke to me about the degree program the college had with a local university. The more he tried to convince me it would be easy for me to get in as I have done at least one year already and all I would need was a bridging year and then one other, I thought this was an amazing opportunity and I would be a fool not to take it, especially as my employer had an agreement with the university to pay all my fees. *It's now or never* I thought and I just went for it.

I was so gassed to start, it felt right and that I could only excel greater by having this but imagine, the person who was adamant she would not go to university, now being excited about the fact that she was accepted onto a degree course. There were other factors to consider, like the classes taking place after work and yes, I had a 2-year-old but this was my time. Needless to say, this journey again was not easy. After my first year, I got pregnant with my second child. I was on a break when I gave birth to him. Then 3 months later, I went back to complete my final year. When they talk about juggling hats, I really did.

I was a mom of 2 boys, a wife, full time assessor who drove up and down the country to visit students. On the weekend my boys would go to my mom's, and I would go to university all day to work on my dissertation. When they told me my dissertation was 13,000 words my mouth dropped! I remember saying 'I don't have all those words in me", but I did, with the help of a Senior Lecturer who helped me to break it down into chunks and encouraged me along the way.

So, on that great day in July 2012, I was awarded with a 2.1 First Class degree in BA Hons in Post Compulsory Education. This is by far one of the greatest achievements of my life outside of getting married and having children.

1. Is the concept of having a 'career' over for good? (ibtimes.co.uk)

Chapter 8
Square Peg, In A Round Hole

In life we are conditioned to believe our success comes from;

GCSEs — A-levels — University

….and, you land the ideal job and are happy!

But guess what, this is not everyone's success story, merely because we are not all academically inclined, or we chose different paths which lead to different opportunities. Who said success only comes from this route? I have known people who haven't gone through all these stages and have become a massive success.

There are no set formulae to being successful. I've seen friends do all the following:

School

A-Levels

University

Still, they do not get a job in the field they studied because of lack of experience. I have seen them fail in school and the moment they leave they find their purpose and thrive. This is my story! I have seen people develop business ideas and are now successful entrepreneurs.

So, it just goes to show we don't all fit in a round hole, we are different. We are diverse and we have creativity in our DNA. It has been proven that experience helps us to excel and also, networking, it's who you know that will often open the door for you to succeed. This is why it's important to not focus on just grades because that is not the be all and end all. The main aim is to never give up, but to keep working towards your goals and dreams until they come to pass.

Just because you left school with the majority of grades under D (or nowadays) 3 and below, that doesn't mean your life ends there. This is your opportunity to re-evaluate your life and decide on where you go next and what will get you to the next destination in life.

As we get older, we develop life skills, skills that will help us get through life easier. This has been taught from our education, so when we leave, we still use these during our next steps. Often for whatever reason, people lack these skills which will lead to unfortunate poor decisions and situations, but I would like to encourage you to develop these skills from now. If you can do voluntary work outside of education, take up hobbies that will enable you to interact with people and learn these skills along the way, or simply take part in after school activities such as Duke of Edinburgh and other sessions, these will allow you to express yourself.

I think there are some essential skills and characteristics you need to focus on to help you excel through life easily and effortlessly:

1. **Communication** – being able to communicate effectively will help you to network and pursue opportunities that can lead you in different experiences.
2. **Innovative** – having ideas to start a business or develop a system or strategy with an existing business will always give you the edge.
3. **Presentation skills** – you should be confident enough to speak to a panel of people or on a one-to-one basis to get your message across; the way you do this must engage your audience and make them want to hear more.
4. **Organisation skills** - this is one of my favourite skills which has come naturally to me over the years. Not everyone has these skills but I hope that everyone has an element of organisation in their life in order to progress and thrive.
5. **Time Management** – Time management works hand in hand with organisation skills, as you will be on time

when you are organised and know where you need to be. Again, an acquired skill which can be developed through practice.

6. **Negotiation** – Negotiation of meaning is a process that speakers go through to reach a clear understanding of each other. For example, asking for clarification, rephrasing, and confirming what you think you have understood, are all strategies for the negotiation of meaning.

I wish to share two stories from two of my friends who have taken different routes. My first friend left school and went into an apprenticeship, she is now a manager within a well-known organisation in the UK:

1. *Can you tell me about your journey from leaving school until where you are today?*

I left high school in May 2005 and went straight into an apprenticeship with the travel agency, 'Thomsons'. My dream career was to become an air stewardess, but the minimum height restriction put a stop to that. This seemed like the perfect alternative, but I hated it. I wanted to interact with customers and find their dream holidays, but I was put on a desk at the back of the shop writing out posters for the front window. I also spent a lot of time taking deliveries of brochures and putting them out in the shop. It was not what I had imagined my travel career to look like, but I guess we have to start somewhere. I was moved to the Wolverhampton store a short time later and after a few months, I knew it wasn't for me and I left.

I found a part-time, temporary job in Matalan. I worked mainly on the home wear department replenishing stock, taking deliveries, doing store moves, preparing for seasonal events and of course, spending time on the tills. I loved being able to interact with people, but I wanted something more permanent and fulfilling.

I saw an apprenticeship advertisement in the local paper for Walsall College. There were a number of vacancies, so I applied. I remember going for an interview in my mum's blouse and some low heel boots I had, feeling very mature. The interview was relaxed, and I was told later that day I was successful. I started in September 2006 on an Intermediate Apprenticeship in Business Administration, based in the Student Services department. I secured a permanent, full-time job after I finished and went on to complete several NVQs before starting my Advanced Apprenticeship in Business Administration. I loved Walsall College. I settled in well and made lots of friends. I spent 16 years at Walsall College, working through departments and courses at full speed and reached my peak when I became the ER Operations Manager for Apprenticeships and Work-based Learning. I had done a full 360 and I was very proud of myself, as were my partner, family and close friends. During the pandemic, I completed a Level 5 Diploma in Leadership and

Management and was able to graduate in May 2022. I had always dreamt of wearing a cap and gown and graduating. This was a massive achievement, I was overjoyed.

Childcare and family commitments changed suddenly in the summer of 2022 which meant I needed to find something part-time. I started looking at job vacancies, but nothing was standing out. A few weeks passed and I saw an opportunity at the local NHS Trust. It was part-time, focused on apprenticeships and the pay was good, considering the reduction in hours. I applied, had an interview via Microsoft Teams and was offered the position the same day.

I started in October 2022 as an Apprenticeship Promotion and Information Officer. I had always aspired to work for a 'brand' and the NHS is one of the best, well-known brands in the UK and across the globe. I am proud to work in the NHS and although not in a clinical role, I am confident that one day another apprenticeship may guide me into that path.

1. *Did you imagine when you started as an apprentice where you might have been now?*

Absolutely not. I never imagined spending 16 years in a company that appointed me as an apprentice when I was 16 years old. I am very grateful for the opportunities I had at Walsall College as they enhanced my career, took me up the ladder and gave me the knowledge, skills and experiences to get me where I am today.

Danielle Wilkes

My second story comes from another friend who completed school, then college and university, here is what she says:

1. **Can you tell me about your journey from leaving school until where you are today?**

My journey from leaving school was taken in small steps at a time.

I had no initial plans to go to university, until I gained good GCSE grades. I worked part-time whilst studying for my A-levels. I was the first one in the family to complete a degree. This was thanks to my English teacher, who encouraged me to consider applying for university. I applied, I visited different campuses and then I picked a course that I thought that I would enjoy. After gaining my A-levels, I was offered a place at the University, where I enjoyed both opportunities and challenges presented to me.

I had the opportunity to work overseas in Atlanta (USA), in 1996 which was the city that hosted the Olympics. I worked for an international festival and had the opportunity to work with upcoming artists such as the Fugees, who are still a well-known music group today. Working with celebrities taught me how to remain humble. Especially when I learnt that my manager was a well-known actor who played a leading role in the film, *Star Trek: Deep Space Nine*. Having a celebrity as a manager was truly a humbling experience for me, for a famous person, he was very inspirational and very down to earth. Even to this day, I like to look out for the other successful artists that I have encountered whilst working for the Arts festival. I remember having to do operational work for The Fugees and had to do errands for one of the lead singers who is credited with breaking many barriers in the music industry. I knew that The Fugees were going to be successful, what I didn't realise was that the band had already become a UK hit, whilst I was in the USA.

I returned to the UK to finish my degree and started to think about the next step of my professional journey. I was interested in teaching, but I wanted to a teach with authenticity and experience, so that I could bring my subjects to life. I decided to head into Customer Service, Sales and Marketing for a manufacturing company.

Handling customers was really challenging, so when I realised that applying customer service skills was better applied within organisations, and was so much more rewarding, I took an opportunity to work as an IT Change Analyst for an international logistics company. This was the start of my IT journey, as I had the great opportunity to learn more about the different IT platforms. I then developed an interest in IT programming and with support from my line manager and peers, I transferred into a technical role and started UNIX programming. It was a great opportunity, and I was still working for the same company, my technical journey continued to progress into project managing international IT projects and travelling.

My manager was based abroad, so even back then I had the experience of working remotely. This was long before the emergence of Covid, as we all now know that the post Covid world has placed us in an era where remote working is now the norm for most companies today.

After getting married and was raising a family, the thought of teaching came back to me, after a successful career in IT. The salary for a teaching assistant wasn't as attractive, so I decided to complete a skills-enhanced course in Computer Science and I also gained a professional teaching qualification. My teaching career covered IT, Computer science, Business Studies, Media Studies and Maths.

I really wanted to help young people see the benefits of education and having a career and linking them both together. Prior to the COVID pandemic in 2020, my colleague and I were approached by a startup company, asking us if we would like to take up the opportunity to help women to get into programming and teach them a range of Computer Science skills. After careful consideration, I took up their offer and I taught remotely for 2 days week and supported the students for rest of the week. I was able to extend my programming skills as I taught and supported a range of programs on other platforms (e.g. Java, C++, Ruby, JavaScript, Agile, Cybersecurity) the company believed in working in an agile environment, so I was learning new skills rapidly.

I have recently taken on an opportunity to head back into the corporate world and now I'm a Senior Technical Trainer for a car manufacturing company. I now provide learning solutions to help trainers and facilitators deliver courses and I develop technical e-learning courses.

My journey from the days of school still continues and currently I have a great opportunity to lead and guide a unique group of professionals who are in the early years of their journey, to help and guide them to experience a smooth professional path.

Over the years I have taken one step at a time and now I can reflect on how successful my career has taken shape since leaving school.

***Did you end up in a job in the industry you studied for? If not, why do you think this is*?**

If anyone would have told me that I would be working for a car manufacturing company 5 years ago, I would have not believed them.

As I have an agile mindset, I appreciate that my current role allows me to utilise all of my skills and experiences to date.

Reflecting on my successes, I now always encourage young professionals to develop their skills and learn more about what they are good at. It is a good thing for those in their early career to follow their heart. So, if you wake up wanting to learn about teeth, consider becoming a dentist. If you are not sure, then do your best in what you enjoy doing and network. Opportunities will present themselves to you.

Natasha Myers

BA Hons Performing Arts with Business Management, PGCE.

2023

Bonus Chapter: For parents and carers

During the past three years I have walked this journey with our firstborn son. To be honest, as a parent, I have always taken my role seriously and especially with education. Maybe because I am a teacher myself and because I know that having the support of your parents along the way makes it easier to go through.

From the moment they got into school (reception) I was present, making sure all homework was completed, attended all parents' evenings, spoke to teachers if I had any concerns or questions.

When 'lock down' happened, our oldest son was in Y8 and I saw his motivation for learning take a nose dive, so I quickly rose to action and had a conversation with him, letting him know he had three more years of school education and I needed him to try his best. Initially, I said we would focus on what is deemed to be the three most important subjects – Maths, English and Sciences. Always at the back of my mind remembering what happened to me and Maths (we were not friends!!!) I signed him up for tuition classes where he would focus on these three. He went constantly every week of course, with much prompting as he never wanted to go, but I always showed him the bigger picture. He stayed in this for eighteen months, but due to his learning style we decided to get him one to one tutoring as opposed to group tutoring, since we knew this would be more beneficial.

It took at least two years for things to get back to normality with lockdowns and time out of school, but when it came to choosing his GCSE options, again we had discussions at length to decide what he wanted to do and why.

One thing, I have always tried to be flexible with my children, understanding that all children are different, and they have different passions and motivations. I knew what my son enjoyed and what would get him out of bed in the morning, so I set my mind to support him in the way that was going to help him work out his career pathway, because yes, it starts as early as Year 9, as this is when they choose their options.

Once his options were in full swing, at the first parents evening, I had a notepad and pen at the ready. I noted down all the exam boards for all subjects he was doing. I also asked the teachers for copies of scheme of works (these are topics they would cover over the year), because if I didn't understand what they were doing, a tutor would and could assist further.

Over the last year, I have physically helped our son in working out a revision schedule, making sure he does it, but also allowing time for him to chill and get some balance. As he has extra curriculum activities, I reduced his midweek session. He still remained attending on weekends so he would have an outlet when studies got too much. I did notice during the start of the year leading up to mock exams that he was very stressed, snappy and not saying much, so I would often take him out for runs or walks to get his mind away from studying. If he had done a few hours, I would book him in for massages so that he could feel relaxed going into his exams.

Parents, we must pay attention to changes in our children, and we have to be supportive to them. Our son knows regardless of what happens end of August, his dad and I support him whatever grades he achieves, because we know he tried his best in them all.

Thankfully, he has a passion to go into Media. We are not sure what area, but earlier this year, he was able to secure a place at a local Sixth Form college to continue his education. He is excited and so are we, as we know he has worked hard to get that place and will continue to work hard in gaining his A levels.

Here are a few key words I want to highlight to you as a parent, which makes the difference.

Be present – make sure the school knows you are interested and concerned with your child/ren's future.

Listen – sometimes instead of talking, just listen to what your child/ren is thinking, feeling or going through.

Advice – you have more experience so share it with your child/ren, don't allow them to make the same mistakes we did - they can do better.

Balance – make sure we allow our child/ren to see or enjoy fun activities even in this difficult time, as it helps them.

Explore – find out their interests and try and help them to get into the field they are looking at, as it makes the transition into the unknown areas easier.

I do understand that some parents feel like they have no idea what's going on in education and that it might be so far away from what you have to do at work, home etc., but when you show interest and give your time, it will encourage your child/ren in all they do. I do understand that you might not have the extra cash to pay for tuition, but again, the internet is full of useful resources to help you and your child/ren.

About the Author and Social Media

Chantel Brooks, QTLS, BA (Hons)

Chantel Brooks is a teacher by profession for over 20 years, an entrepreneur and author who specialises in Business and Event Management. She has chaired and served on boards both in the private and voluntary sectors. Currently, Chantel is Chair of the board for a multi-academy trust local secondary school. Chantel has years of experience in project management, event management, as well as general business leadership and this is what she currently lectures in. Chantel has been able to exercise the theory with practise by running her own business.

Chantel has won an award for wedding consultant of the year and within her academic achievements, seen a number of students achieve 'grade 9' (A*) in Business Studies GCSE. In her pursuit to educate young people about entrepreneurship she has mentored over 5 young people who have created businesses from her sessions.

Chantel has launched a franchise of Ultra Education in Birmingham, teaching young people ages 7-17 years about entrepreneurship. She regularly gives back to the community through supporting local schools and churches with her skills in fundraising and organising large events. Chantel is a renowned speaker who has delivered workshops for ladies and young people across the United Kingdom.

Please feel free to contact me on either my website or social media:

Website: www.chantelbrooks.co.uk

Instagram – @officialchantelbrooks

Facebook – Chantel Brooks

Twitter- @chantelbrooks

Linkedin – Chantel Brooks

Snapchat – @ChantelBrooks

Tiktok - @officialchantelbrooks

Milton Keynes UK
Ingram Content Group UK Ltd.
UKHW021018240823
427411UK00010B/285

9 781399 961615